When I'm Feeling

ANGRY

Written and illustrated by Trace Moroney

GINGHAM DOG
PRESS

Columbus, Ohio

When I'm feeling angry,
I feel like there is a boiling hot
volcano in my tummy
that is about to...

expl

When I'm feeling angry,
I want to kick and scream and

stomp,  **stomp,**

stomp my feet so hard
that the whole world shakes.

I want to run and run and never stop!

Everyone gets angry sometimes.

Some things make me
really angry.

I feel angry
when someone
makes fun
of me

or ruins something that I made.

I feel angry when I'm blamed
for something that I didn't do.

It's okay to feel angry

as long as my anger doesn't hurt anyone else.

When I'm feeling angry, I try to do things that make me feel better.

I take great big breaths

in   and   out

or
I go
to my
favorite
quiet
place.

Talking about why I'm angry
with someone who cares about me
helps to make some of my anger go away.

Sometimes I am *soooo* angry
that I forget why I was angry
in the first place.

And that
makes
me
laugh!

Think About It!

1. What does the little rabbit do when it feels angry?

2. What kinds of things make the little rabbit angry?

3. How do you know when the little rabbit is feeling angry?

4. What does the little rabbit do to feel better?

The Story and You!

1. What kinds of things make you feel angry?

2. What do you do when you feel angry?

3. On a separate piece of paper, draw a picture of something that makes you feel angry.

4. What makes you feel better?

For my sister, Sarah

Text and illustration copyright © Trace Moroney
First published in Australia by The Five Mile Press Pty Ltd.
Printed in China.
This edition published in the United States in 2006 by
Gingham Dog Press, an imprint of School Specialty
Publishing, a member of the School Specialty Family.

Library of Congress Cataloging-in-Publication Data is on file
with the publisher.

Send all inquiries to:

School Specialty Publishing
8720 Orion Place
Columbus, OH 43240-2111

ISBN 0-7696-4424-4

1 2 3 4 5 6 7 8 9 FMP 10 09 08 07 06 05

www.SchoolSpecialtyPublishing.com